The Usborne
Little
Encyclopedia
of
Space

Paul Dowswell

Designed by Keith Newell & Helen Wood

Illustrated by Gary Bines & David Hancock

Space consultant: Stuart Atkinson
Managing designer: Mary Cartwright
Managing editor: Felicity Brooks
Digital manipulation: John Russell, Mike Olley & Roger Bolton
Picture research: Ruth King
Cover design: Hannah Ahmed

Using Internet links

Throughout this book we have suggested interesting websites where you can find out more about space. To visit the sites, go to the Usborne Quicklinks Website at **www.usborne-quicklinks.com** and type the keywords "little space". Here are some of the things you can do on the websites:

- Take a tour of the Solar System
- See pictures from the Hubble Space Telescope
- Find out how astronauts train for space flights
- Take a tour of the International Space Station
- Search for alien life forms

Internet safety

When using the Internet, please make sure you follow these guidelines:

- Ask your parent's or guardian's permission before you connect to the Internet.
- If you write a message in a website guest book or on a website message board, do not include any personal information such as your full name, address or telephone number, and ask an adult before you give your email address.
- Never arrange to meet anyone you have talked to on the Internet.
- If a website asks you to log in or register by typing your name or email address, ask permission from an adult first.
- If you do receive an email from someone you don't know, tell an adult and do not reply to the email.

Computer not essential

If you don't have access to the Internet, don't worry. This book is a complete, self-contained reference book on its own.

Site availability

The links in Usborne Quicklinks are regularly reviewed and updated, but occasionally, you may get a message that a site is unavailable. This might be temporary, so try again later, or even the next day. Websites do occasionally close down and when this happens, we will replace them with new links in Usborne Quicklinks. Sometimes we add extra links too, if we think they are useful. So when you visit Usborne Quicklinks, the links may be slightly different from those described in your book.

Downloadable pictures

Pictures in this book marked with a ★ symbol can be downloaded from Usborne Quicklinks for your own personal use, for example, to illustrate a homework report or project. The pictures are the copyright of Usborne Publishing and may not be used for any commercial or profit-related purpose. To download a picture, go to Usborne Quicklinks and follow the instructions there.

Notes for parents and guardians

The websites described in this book are regularly reviewed and the links in Usborne Quicklinks are updated. However, the content of a website may change at any time and Usborne Publishing is not responsible for the content on any website other than its own. We recommend that children are supervised while on the Internet, that they do not use Internet chat rooms, and that you use Internet filtering software to block unsuitable material. Please ensure that your children read and follow the safety guidelines printed on the left. For more information, see the "Net Help" area on the Usborne Quicklinks Website.

To go to all the websites described in this book, go to **www.usborne-quicklinks.com** and enter the keywords "little space".

Contents

Amazing space

Space is full of amazing sights. Some you can see with your own eyes, or with a telescope or binoculars. Here are some of the things you can find out about in this part of the book.

Spacecraft

Rockets have been going into space since 1957. They have taken people as far as the Moon. Spacecraft without people in them have visited distant planets such as Uranus and Neptune.

This American rocket is taking three people to the Moon.

Astronauts

People who travel into space are called astronauts. They have to train for many years before their trip.

This astronaut wears a space suit to "walk" in space. ★

Stars

A star is a blazing ball of very hot gas. The Sun is a star.

Below you can see new stars being made from clouds of dust.

The planet
Neptune

Moons

Most planets have
moons. These are
mini-planets
which travel
around other
planets.

This is Io, one of
Jupiter's moons.

Planets

A planet is an enormous ball of rock or
gas which travels around a star. A group
of planets moving around a star is known
as a solar system.

The planet Saturn

Comets

Comets are balls of dirty
ice, which fly around in
space. Sometimes they
crash into planets.

This is
a comet. ★

Galaxies

Galaxies are huge groups of stars. Our
Sun and its solar system are in a galaxy
called the Milky Way. Scientists think
there are billions of galaxies in space.

This galaxy is called
the Sombrero Galaxy.
It has millions of stars.

5

The moving sky

Everything in the Universe, from little moons to entire solar systems and galaxies, is moving. Even if you are sitting very still to read this book, you are still moving through space at 1,000km (600 miles) a second.

Spinners

All planets and moons spin around. Earth spins at roughly 1,600kph (1,000mph). It takes 24 hours to go all the way around. We measure our day by this amount of time.

This photo of stars was made over several hours. The position of the stars has changed in the sky because the Earth is spinning around.

Night and day

As Earth turns, the part that faces the Sun is lit up, and the part that faces away from the Sun is dark. This is why we have day and night.

The Earth keeps turning as it travels around the Sun. It takes 365 days (one year) to go once around the Sun.

It is still dark in North America.

1

7:00am
Sun rises over Europe.

Sun is rising in North America.

2

12:00 noon
Sun is high in the sky in Europe.

3

7:00pm
Sun has gone down in Europe.

Sun is high in the sky in North America.

Big circles

As they spin, planets and moons move through space in huge circular paths called orbits. It is hard to see them moving as they seem to travel slowly, like the hour hand on a watch.

The yellow lines and arrows in the pictures on the right show the paths a planet and a moon take in their orbits.

A planet orbits around a sun.

A moon orbits around a planet.

Gravity

Planets stay in orbit around the Sun, instead of flying off into space, because of a force called gravity. Everything in the Universe is held together by gravity. It pulls every object toward every other object.

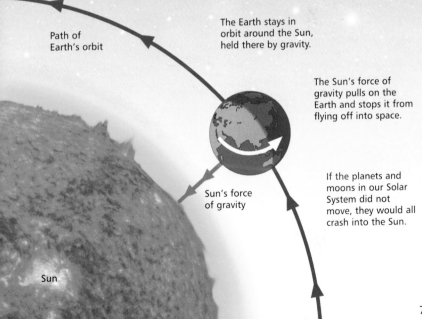

Path of Earth's orbit

The Earth stays in orbit around the Sun, held there by gravity.

The Sun's force of gravity pulls on the Earth and stops it from flying off into space.

Sun's force of gravity

If the planets and moons in our Solar System did not move, they would all crash into the Sun.

Sun

Telescopes

Telescopes make things look bigger. Ever since they were invented 400 years ago, astronomers have been using them to find out more about space.

How a telescope works

A telescope uses a curved glass circle called a lens to magnify (make larger) objects. The first astronomer to use a telescope was an Italian man named Galileo. His telescope made stars and planets look three times bigger.

A replica of Galileo's telescope

Lens

Lens

Hollow tube

Light comes in here.

Galileo used a telescope to discover rings around Saturn.

Modern telescopes

Today, astronomers use curved mirrors in telescopes, as well as glass lenses. These give better images. Big astronomy telescopes are placed high on mountains. The air is clearer there, so there is a better view of the sky.

This is the Kitt Peak Observatory in Arizona, USA.

The telescope inside this tower is called the Mayall Telescope. It is one of the biggest in the world. It looks at distant galaxies and nebulas.

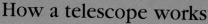

Space telescope

A big telescope called the Hubble Space Telescope orbits the Earth. It is outside the haze and pollution of our planet's atmosphere*, so it is able to take incredibly clear photographs of the Universe.

Internet link

For a link to a website where you can see pictures from the Hubble Space Telescope, go to **www.usborne-quicklinks.com**

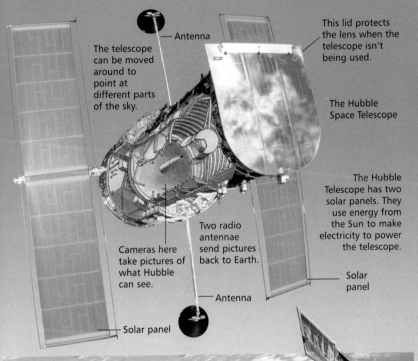

— Antenna

The telescope can be moved around to point at different parts of the sky.

This lid protects the lens when the telescope isn't being used.

The Hubble Space Telescope

The Hubble Telescope has two solar panels. They use energy from the Sun to make electricity to power the telescope.

Two radio antennae send pictures back to Earth.

Cameras here take pictures of what Hubble can see.

Solar panel

— Antenna

Solar panel

Hubble Telescope

Astronauts

Space shuttle —

Space repairs

When the Hubble Space Telescope was first put into space in 1990 it didn't work properly. Three years later, some astronauts went up in a space shuttle to repair it. Now the telescope sends back very clear pictures.

*See page 29 for more about Earth's atmosphere.

9

Radio telescopes

In space there are billions of things that are too dark or far away for an ordinary telescope to look at. A radio telescope can find things an ordinary telescope can't. This is because it does not use light to "see".

Star signals

Stars and other space objects all give off some kind of signal which shows that they are there. This may be light, heat or sound. It may also be another type of signal called a radio wave. This is what a radio telescope picks up.

This is a galaxy called Centaurus A. Like all galaxies it is giving off radio waves that travel through space.

A radio telescope picks up these radio waves. It sends them to a computer, to be turned into a picture.

This is a computer picture of radio waves from Centaurus A.

Radio waves

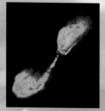

Unlike light telescopes, radio telescopes can be used during the day as well as at night.

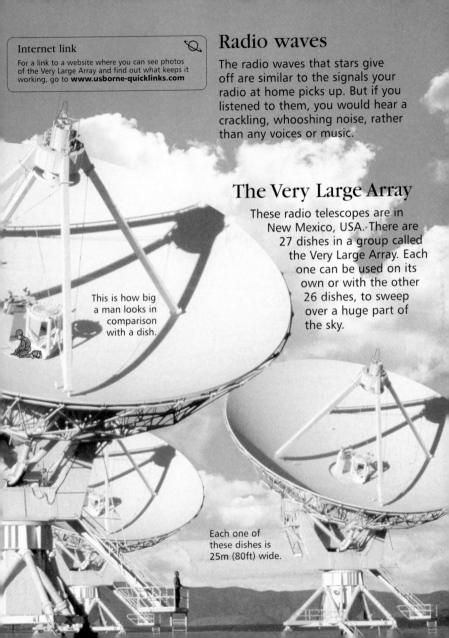

Internet link

For a link to a website where you can see photos of the Very Large Array and find out what keeps it working, go to **www.usborne-quicklinks.com**

Radio waves

The radio waves that stars give off are similar to the signals your radio at home picks up. But if you listened to them, you would hear a crackling, whooshing noise, rather than any voices or music.

The Very Large Array

These radio telescopes are in New Mexico, USA. There are 27 dishes in a group called the Very Large Array. Each one can be used on its own or with the other 26 dishes, to sweep over a huge part of the sky.

This is how big a man looks in comparison with a dish.

Each one of these dishes is 25m (80ft) wide.

Trips into space

People have only been sending rockets into space since 1957. Before then, rockets fell back to the ground before they could reach space. They were not powerful enough to go any farther.

The space shuttle

The first people went into space in 1961. Since then hundreds of men and women have followed them. Today, astronauts fly into space in a rocket called a space shuttle. This is how it works.

Tailfin

When it returns from space, the shuttle's wings help it to glide back to Earth.

Astronauts have to wear spacesuits to go into the cargo bay or outside the space shuttle.

Booster rocket

Fuel tank

1. The shuttle blasts off from Earth.

2. Two booster rockets fall away when their fuel runs out, and parachute back to Earth.

3. The main engine takes the shuttle into space. The big fuel tank falls away when it's empty.

USA

NASA Endeavour

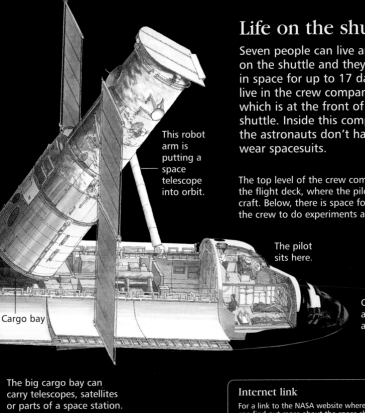

Life on the shuttle

Seven people can live and work on the shuttle and they can stay in space for up to 17 days. They live in the crew compartment which is at the front of the shuttle. Inside this compartment the astronauts don't have to wear spacesuits.

The top level of the crew compartment is the flight deck, where the pilot flies the craft. Below, there is space for the rest of the crew to do experiments and sleep.

This robot arm is putting a space telescope into orbit.

The pilot sits here.

Cargo bay

Can you see a sleeping astronaut?

The big cargo bay can carry telescopes, satellites or parts of a space station.

Internet link

For a link to the NASA website where you can find out more about the space shuttle, go to **www.usborne-quicklinks.com**

4. On its return, the shuttle glides back through the Earth's atmosphere. Its underside gets very hot.

5. The shuttle touches down. It lands on wheels like a plane.

United States

Astronaut training

Astronauts train for years to prepare for a trip into space. Here you can see some of the ways they do this at an astronaut training school in Houston, Texas, USA.

Which button do I press?

A space shuttle pilot steers the spaceship from a control panel which looks like the one below. There are hundreds of buttons to press. Astronauts learn how to control a shuttle in a machine called a flight simulator.

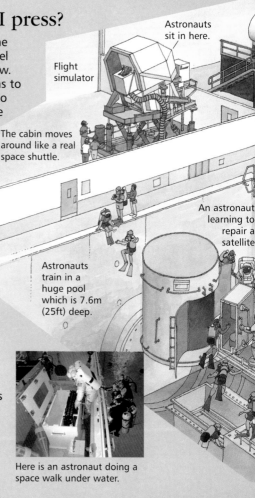

Astronauts sit in here.

Flight simulator

The cabin moves around like a real space shuttle.

An astronaut learning to repair a satellite

Astronauts train in a huge pool which is 7.6m (25ft) deep.

This is what it looks like ★ inside a flight simulator. Television screens show what the real view would be like.

Floating around

In space everything floats. This is called being weightless and it is a very strange feeling. Astronauts get used to it by training under water, which is the nearest thing on Earth to being weightless.

Here is an astronaut doing a space walk under water.

Making a quick escape

Astronauts must learn how to get out of their space shuttle quickly during an emergency at take-off or landing. In the photo on the right you can see an astronaut trying out an escape when the shuttle has landed back on Earth.

Robot arm

This astronaut is sliding down a rope to escape from the space shuttle.

This is a full-scale model of the space shuttle's cargo bay. This is where astronauts learn to use the shuttle's robot arm, which moves satellites in or out of the cargo bay.

Divers help the astronauts if they get into trouble.

Taking the "Vomit Comet"

Astronauts can also learn how it feels to be weightless by flying in a jet which takes a steep climb. At the top of the climb they are weightless for 30 seconds. People feel sick sometimes, so the plane is nicknamed the "Vomit Comet".

Here are astronauts floating around in the plane. There is lots of padding to stop them from getting hurt.

Internet link

For a link to a website with virtual astronaut training exercises and video clips, go to
www.usborne-quicklinks.com

15

A walk in space

Space is deadly. There is no air to breathe, so outside a spacecraft, an astronaut must wear an outfit called a spacesuit to stay alive. Spacesuits are like body-size spaceships, with their own air and water supplies.

A spacesuit has several very thin but strong layers. These protect the astronaut from tiny meteoroids, and the heat and cold of space.

A camera on the helmet films what the astronaut is doing.

Because his face is hidden by his helmet, this stripe shows other astronauts who is in this spacesuit.

Lights on the helmet help the astronaut to see in the dark.

The suit is flexible enough to allow easy movement.

The astronaut can control the equipment in a spacesuit from this unit.

Walk to work

Astronauts make space walks to repair satellites, build space stations or check the outside of their spaceships. On these pages you can see two American astronauts making a space walk from their space shuttle in 1997.

Internet link

For a link to the NASA website where there is a history of human space flight, go to **www.usborne-quicklinks.com**

Survival equipment

Here is some of the equipment astronauts need to stay alive and comfortable outside their spaceships. Sometimes space walks can last for five hours or more.

The shiny visor of the helmet protects against blinding, bright sunlight.

This cap holds a radio microphone and ear piece in place.

A drink bag has a tube which goes straight to the astronaut's mouth.

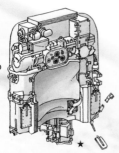

This is the "Primary Life Support System". It contains air for the astronaut to breathe.

This outfit is worn next to the body. It has tubes of water which the astronaut can make hot or cold, to warm up or cool down.

Padded gloves have rubber fingertips so the astronaut can feel things more easily.

Boiling and freezing

When astronauts on a space walk face the Sun, its rays are hotter than boiling water. But when their spaceships travel around the dark side of the Earth, temperatures drop way below freezing.

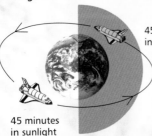

A space shuttle takes 90 minutes to go around the Earth.

45 minutes in darkness

45 minutes in sunlight

Living in space

Space stations are homes in space where astronauts can look at the Earth and do experiments. People can live in them for many months at a time. The first space station was set up over 30 years ago.

The ISS

This is the International Space Station (ISS). It floats 370km (230 miles) above the Earth with three people on board. The first crew arrived in 2000. A space shuttle takes them up and back to Earth. The station is still being built, but when it is finished, seven or more people could live there.

This is the inside of a laboratory where scientists can do tests to see how things behave in space.

★

Internet link

For a link to a website where you can take a virtual tour of the International Space Station, go to **www.usborne-quicklinks.com**

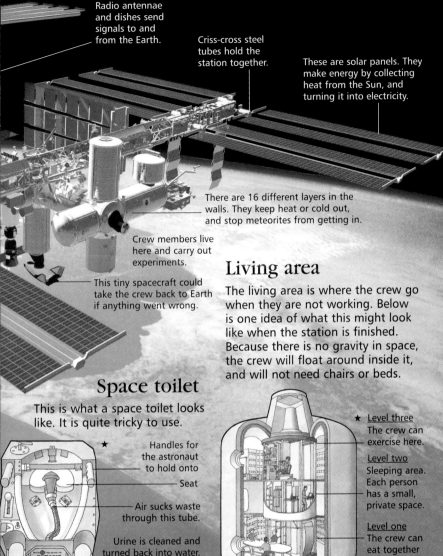

Radio antennae and dishes send signals to and from the Earth.

Criss-cross steel tubes hold the station together.

These are solar panels. They make energy by collecting heat from the Sun, and turning it into electricity.

There are 16 different layers in the walls. They keep heat or cold out, and stop meteorites from getting in.

Crew members live here and carry out experiments.

This tiny spacecraft could take the crew back to Earth if anything went wrong.

Living area

The living area is where the crew go when they are not working. Below is one idea of what this might look like when the station is finished. Because there is no gravity in space, the crew will float around inside it, and will not need chairs or beds.

Space toilet

This is what a space toilet looks like. It is quite tricky to use.

★ Handles for the astronaut to hold onto

Seat

Air sucks waste through this tube.

Urine is cleaned and turned back into water. Solid waste is frozen and returned to Earth.

★ Level three
The crew can exercise here.

Level two
Sleeping area. Each person has a small, private space.

Level one
The crew can eat together around this big table.

19

Dangers and disasters

Going into space can be very dangerous. Astronauts only survive because their spaceship or spacesuit protects them. The most dangerous parts of the journey are the take-off, and return to Earth.

When the space shuttle Challenger's main fuel tank caught fire, it caused this massive explosion.

Shuttle explosion

One of the worst ever space disasters happened in 1986. A space shuttle named Challenger exploded only 90 seconds after taking off. All seven of the astronauts on board the shuttle died.

The Challenger space shuttle taking off

Fuel leaking from here caught fire.

Lucky Apollo 13

In 1970, three astronauts were going to the Moon in a spacecraft named Apollo 13. Halfway there, part of the spacecraft blew up. Some of the fuel supply had exploded. The crew survived the disaster, but almost ran out of air on the way back to Earth.

An explosion here nearly destroyed Apollo 13.

Internet link

For a link to a website where you can try and land on the Moon without crashing, go to **www.usborne-quicklinks.com**

The astronauts escaped into this part of Apollo 13.

One whole side of the spaceship blew away.

The astronauts made this box from storage bags, tape and air hoses to clean their air.

Up in smoke

The European Space Agency launched its first Ariane 5 rocket in 1996. But a computer on board did not work properly. Less than a minute after take-off, Ariane 5 began to fly in the wrong direction. Then it broke into pieces and exploded.

Ariane 5 taking off

Satellites and space probes

Satellites and space probes are spaceships with no people in them. Instead, scientists control them from Earth. Most satellites and probes have cameras or other kinds of viewing equipment.

This is the European Remote Sensing Satellite, known as ERS. It can take very detailed pictures of the Earth.

Satellites

Some satellites look down on Earth and others look out into space. Other types of satellites are used to carry television pictures or phone messages around the world. ★

Solar panels

This is the SOHO satellite, which looks at the atmosphere of the Sun. It is also used to find out about the solar wind (see page 32).

Space probes

Space probes do similar jobs to satellites, but instead of orbiting the Earth, they visit other planets. All the planets have been visited, except for Pluto. Sometimes space probes even land on other planets.

The painting on the right shows the Voyager space probe heading toward Neptune in 1989.

Internet link

For a link to a website where you can learn more about satellites, go to www.usborne-quicklinks.com

Space views

Here are two pictures taken by satellites. Special cameras are used to show particular details, which can also be made clearer with computers.

This ERS picture shows a hole in Antarctica's atmosphere.

This SOHO picture shows the outer edge of the Sun's surface.

A big picture

A satellite named COBE took the picture below. It is a temperature map of the entire universe.

Some parts of space are hotter than others. The red and blue areas show different temperatures.

COBE satellite

23

Into the future

Going into space is very expensive, so what happens in the future depends on how much money countries want to spend on exploring space. Here are some of the things that might happen over the next hundred years.

Spaceships such as this could visit Mars then return to Earth.

Mission to Mars

Space probes have landed on Mars, taken pictures and carried out experiments. There are now plans for a robot spaceship to visit the planet and return to Earth with samples of soil and rock. People could visit Mars within 20 years, if there is enough money for the trip. Space bases may be built there too, in about 50 years' time.

A base on Mars might look like this.

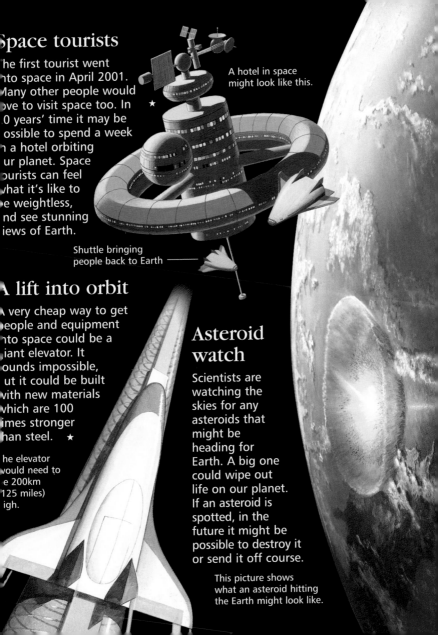

Space tourists

The first tourist went into space in April 2001. Many other people would love to visit space too. In 10 years' time it may be possible to spend a week in a hotel orbiting our planet. Space tourists can feel what it's like to be weightless, and see stunning views of Earth.

A hotel in space might look like this.

Shuttle bringing people back to Earth ———

A lift into orbit

A very cheap way to get people and equipment into space could be a giant elevator. It sounds impossible, but it could be built with new materials which are 100 times stronger than steel. ★

The elevator would need to be 200km (125 miles) high.

Asteroid watch

Scientists are watching the skies for any asteroids that might be heading for Earth. A big one could wipe out life on our planet. If an asteroid is spotted, in the future it might be possible to destroy it or send it off course.

This picture shows what an asteroid hitting the Earth might look like.

Is anyone out there?

Ever since people first began to study the stars, they have wondered whether there is life in space. At the moment we don't know. Some astronomers think we will find evidence of alien life before the end of the century.

Reaching out

Two kinds of space probes are heading out of our Solar System. Pioneer probes carry a picture of people and a map that shows where Earth is. Voyagers carry a disc with sounds and pictures of Earth. These are to show any alien who may find them what we look like.

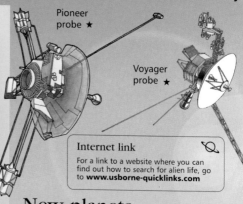

Pioneer probe ★

Voyager probe ★

Internet link

For a link to a website where you can find out how to search for alien life, go to **www.usborne-quicklinks.com**

New planets

Recently, astronomers have discovered new planets in orbit around stars. Perhaps there is life there. Radio telescopes, such as the one i Puerto Rico shown below, search the skies near these planets, looking for alien signals.

Arecibo radio telescope is the largest in the world.

The Voyager disc

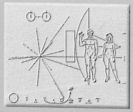

The Pioneer map and picture

Life on Europa?

Europa, one of Jupiter's moons, has an icy surface. Under it there may be a cold, dark sea. Scientists think they may find creatures there, perhaps like those that live deep under water on Earth. A space probe may go to visit Europa in the future to try to find out more.

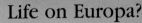

Europa

In the future, submarine probes from Earth may explore under the ice of Europa.

What might aliens look like?

If we do find life in space, it may not look very interesting. It could be slime or moss, rather than intelligent creatures with arms, legs and heads, like us.

Some scientists think germ-like blobs found in a rock from Mars show life existed there.

Aliens may look like this in films, but we don't really know what they might look like.
★

What's in our Solar System?

Our Solar System is the Sun and everything that revolves around it. It includes all the planets and their moons, and space objects such as comets. There are also two vast bands of drifting rocks called the Asteroid Belt and the Kuiper Belt.

In this picture of the Solar System the planets are not shown to scale.

Comets fly around the Solar System.

Days and years

A day is the time it takes for a planet to spin around once. Earth's day lasts 24 hours. A year is the time it takes for a planet to go all the way around the Sun. Earth's year lasts for 365 days.

Earth

A day

Sun

A year

Asteroid Belt

Saturn is the second biggest planet.

Neptune is a gas planet, like Jupiter, Saturn, and Uranus. The gas planets are all much bigger than the rocky planets in our Solar System.

Internet link

For a link to a website where you can
take an incredible tour of the Solar System,
go to **www.usborne-quicklinks.com**

Jupiter
is the
biggest
planet.

Venus

Mercury

The Sun

Mars

Earth

Atmosphere

Most planets have an
atmosphere – a layer
of gas that covers the
surface. Earth's
atmosphere is made
of air. It stretches
400km (250 miles)
above us. It provides
air to breathe, and
helps protect us from
the Sun's heat.

Earth's atmosphere

Uranus spins
on its side. It
has rings like
Saturn.

Pluto is a tiny,
rocky planet.

Beyond Pluto lies a band
of icy rocks named
the Kuiper Belt.

The Moon

The Moon travels around the Earth, just like the Earth travels around the Sun. So far, the Moon is the only part of the Solar System that people have been able to visit.

Sea of Crises

The Moon's "seas" are actually dark patches of melted rock.

Sea of Tranquillity

Craters were made by rocks from space, crashing into the Moon.

Sea of Serenity

Apollo 15 landed here in 1971.

Sea of Rain

Earth

If you were orbiting the Moon in a spaceship, this is how far away Earth would look.

When people went to the Moon between 1969 and 1972, it took their spaceships three days to get there.

What is the Moon like?

The Moon is very different from Earth. There is no air, no weather, and no life. It is a dreary, dusty place that is boiling hot by day and freezing at night. The surface is covered with saucer-shaped holes called craters. You can see some if you look at the Moon on a clear night. Some are so huge, a city the size of London could fit inside them.

Where did the Moon come from?

The Moon is about the same age as the Earth. Here is one idea about where it came from.

1. Soon after the Earth formed, a planet hit it. ★

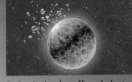

2. Rocks broke off and shot into space. ★

3. The rocks were held in ★ orbit by Earth's gravity.

4. These rocks slowly formed into the Moon. ★

Moon landings

People have visited the Moon six times, but not since 1972. Each spaceship that landed there carried two astronauts. They stayed up to three days before returning.

Internet link

For a link to a website where you can find out more about Moon landings, go to **www.usborne-quicklinks.com**

The astronaut is saluting the American flag.

This spaceship is called a lunar module.

This is the Apollo 15 Moon landing. See where they are on the Moon, on the facing page.

Car powered by electricity

The Sun

The Sun is a star. It is a huge ball of blazing gas that makes vast amounts of light and heat which we call sunshine. It is so big it could hold a million planets the size of Earth. It looks like it's burning, but it's actually exploding like a massive bomb.

The Sun's surface is called the photosphere. The temperature there is 5,500ºC (10,000ºF). The dark areas are sunspots. The temperature is lower there.

The size of the Earth, compared to the Sun

> **Internet link**
>
> For a link to the NASA website where you can find out more about the Sun, go to **www.usborne-quicklinks.com**

The solar wind

As well as light and heat, the Sun also sends out a stream of invisible specks, called particles, into space. This is called the solar wind. When the particles pass by the North and South Poles of Earth they can make the air glow beautiful reds, blues, greens and purples.

This is the solar wind lighting up the sky near the North Pole.

This is a solar prominence. It is a massive arch of hot gas, which reaches out into space like a huge, flaming tongue.

Solar surface

The Sun makes sunlight by burning four million tonnes (tons) of fuel every second. You can see in this picture that the Sun's surface is a churning mass of explosions. Solar flares and fiery loops of gas leap out into space.

The photo on the right shows a close-up of the Sun's surface. You can see jets of gas called plasma loops.

Liquid, ice or gas?

Life exists on Earth because our planet is just the right distance from the Sun for water to be a liquid, rather than ice or a gas.

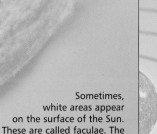

Mars is too cold.

Venus is too hot.

Sun

Earth is just right.

★

Sometimes, white areas appear on the surface of the Sun. These are called faculae. The temperature here is even higher than that of the rest of the Sun.

Mercury and Venus

Mercury and Venus are the two planets closest to the Sun. Both are small and very hot. Mercury has almost no atmosphere, but Venus is covered with a thick layer of gas.

Tiny Mercury

Mercury is a tiny planet. Billions of years ago many rocks crashed into it, so its surface is covered with lots of craters. Because it is so close to the Sun, it has the shortest year of any planet. Mercury takes just 88 Earth days to travel around the Sun.

Mercury is a third the size of Earth, but is almost as heavy. It has a core of dense metal. This makes up nearly three-quarters of its inside.

Crust

Mercury

Metal core

Four billion years ago, an enormous meteorite crashed into Mercury. It made a massive crater called the Caloris Basin. This is more than 1,250km (800 miles) across.

Meteorite hitting Mercury

Internet links
For links to the NASA website where you can see more pictures of Mercury and Venus, go to
www.usborne-quicklinks.com

Beneath its clouds, Venus is a world of volcanoes, mountains and canyons. The pink and white areas on this computer picture show high, rough areas. Low, flat ground is shown in green.

Sweltering Venus

Venus is the nearest planet to us. Although it is farther away from the Sun than Mercury, its surface is actually hotter. This is because it has a thick atmosphere of the gas carbon dioxide. This atmosphere traps the Sun's heat and keeps it from escaping back into space.

★

Magellan probe

The picture below shows the surface of Venus. It was taken by the Magellan probe which visited Venus between 1990 and 1994.

Mars

If you were standing on Mars, being there would be a little like being on Earth. There is a bright sky during the day, and you could see thin clouds, morning mists and light frosts. But Mars is a lot colder than our planet.

Mars in detail

Mars is half the size of Earth. It is covered mainly with rocks and dust. Most of it looks like a great big desert. It has a thin atmosphere of poisonous gas.

Internet link

For a link to a website where you can explore Mars and NASA's latest mission to the red planet, go to **www.usborne-quicklinks.com**

This is a polar ice cap where water has frozen into a huge field of ice.

These marks are great fields of dark dust. They are blown around by fierce storms.

This is a volcano called Olympus Mons.

This is a volcano called Ascraeus Mons.

This is a huge canyon called The Valles Marineris.

The Viking 1 space probe visited Mars in 1976. It sent down the first craft to land on the surface.

Volcanoes and canyons

Mars has some very interesting features. There are several volcanoes. The biggest one is called Olympus Mons. It is the largest in the Solar System. It rises 25km (15 miles) above the surface of Mars. There are also huge canyons and dried-up water channels.

The Olympus Mons volcano seen by a visiting space probe.

The Valles Marineris canyon is a huge crack along one side of the planet. It is so long it would stretch across the whole of the USA.

Channels

Astronomers think that channels like this were made by running water, which has now frozen or leaked away.

Visitors to Mars

The photograph below shows the surface of Mars. It was taken by the Pathfinder space probe, which landed there in 1997. On board was a little mobile robot called Sojourner. It carried TV cameras and could be moved around by scientists on Earth.

Scientists think that the rocks you can see in this picture were left here by a big flood, billions of years ago.

The Sojourner robot is the size of a microwave oven. This picture shows some of its more important features:

A Solar panels make power from sunlight.
B Small wheels with studded rims grip the surface.
C Radio antenna keeps the robot in contact with Earth.
D A camera and laser are used to help steer the robot.

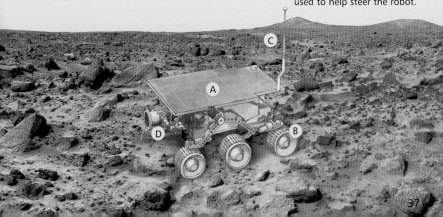

Jupiter and Saturn

Beyond the Asteroid Belt lie four huge planets that are mainly made up of gas. The largest of these four are the bright, stormy planets Jupiter and Saturn.

Swirly world

Jupiter is the biggest planet in the Solar System and has at least 61 moons. It also has the shortest day. It takes only 9 hours and 50 minutes to spin around once. Jupiter is a stormy planet. Swirling clouds of gas race around it, in dark and light bands.

The Great Red Spot is a storm three times the size of Earth.

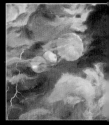

A pod from the Galileo space probe parachuted into Jupiter's gassy atmosphere in 1995.

This space probe photo shows thick, hot gas erupting from volcanoes on the surface of Io, one of Jupiter's many moons.

Internet links

For links to websites where you can find out more about Jupiter and Saturn, go to **www.usborne-quicklinks.com**

Ring world

Saturn is the second biggest
planet in the Solar System.
Many broad rings of rock
and ice orbit around it.
Saturn is very light. If
you could put it in a
huge swimming
pool, it would
float there.

All shapes and sizes

The rocks in Saturn's rings may have come from one of its moons.
You can see what might have happened below. Some rocks in the
rings are as big as a house, others are smaller than a pebble.

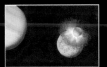

A moon collided
with a planet.

It broke into
billions of pieces.

The pieces stayed
in Saturn's orbit.

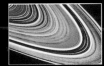

Eventually, they
formed Saturn's rings.

Saturn's moons

Saturn has 31 moons, and there
may be more. Titan is the largest.
It has a thick atmosphere.

Here you can see
how big Titan is
compared to the
planet Mercury
and our Moon.

This picture shows
what Titan's atmosphere
may look like, close up.

Titan

The planet
Mercury

Earth's
Moon

Uranus and Neptune

Uranus and Neptune are huge gas planets. Both are around four times bigger than Earth. They are hard to spot in the night sky, but you can see them with a telescope.

Uranus   Neptune   Earth

This is how big Uranus and Neptune are compared to the Earth.

Uranus

This world spins on its side. Its outer surface is cloaked by a thin mist, which wraps around a thick gassy surface. Further inside, Uranus has a core of solid rock.

Here are some of Uranus's moons.

Umbriel

Ariel

Titania

Oberon

Uranus

Puzzle moon

Uranus has 21 moons. One of them, Miranda, looks like a huge jigsaw puzzle. Perhaps, millions of years ago, it broke into pieces. Gradually time and gravity put it back together.

Miranda

★

A comet may have crashed into Miranda.

★

Miranda's pieces drifted together.

★

Miranda slowly put itself back into one piece.

This is what Miranda's surface looks like now.

Neptune

Neptune has the worst storms in the Solar System. Winds of 2,000kph (1,250mph) whip methane clouds around the planet.

Neptune has twelve moons. One, named Triton, is a frozen world. Ice on its surface acts like a greenhouse, magnifying the Sun's feeble rays, and heating gas that lies beneath. This causes hot jets of gas and slush to spout out through the ice and into space.

Internet link ✎

For a link to a website where you can find out more about Uranus and Neptune, go to **www.usborne-quicklinks.com**

Triton orbits in the opposite direction from all of Neptune's other moons.

Visitor from Earth

The Voyager 2 space probe visited Uranus and Neptune in 1986 and 1989. The probe took 12 years to get to Neptune from Earth.

★

Voyager 2

This picture shows what the surface of Triton might look like. A jet of gas and slush is spouting out.

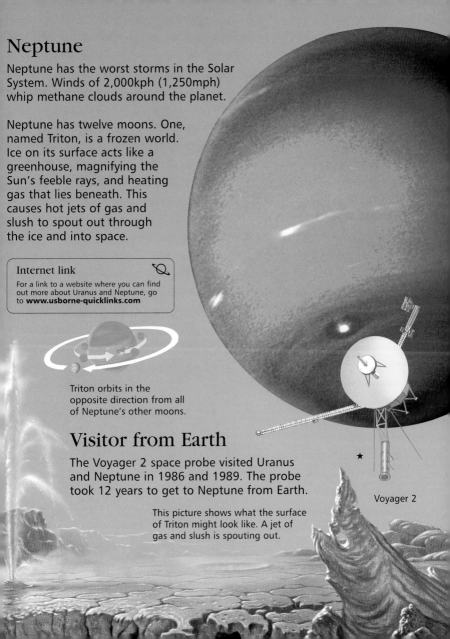

Pluto and beyond

Pluto lies at the very edge of the Solar System. The planet is so far away it was only discovered in 1930. Unlike the gassy planets Uranus and Neptune, Pluto is a solid ball of rock and ice.

Moon-sized

Pluto's moon, Charon

Pluto is a tiny planet. It is smaller than our Moon. Both Pluto, and its moon Charon, could fit into the borders of the USA. Some astronomers think Pluto is an asteroid, and not a planet.

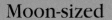

Pluto

A space probe would take 12 years to get to Pluto. No probe has visited it yet, but one may in the future.

Pluto may have a thin atmosphere of nitrogen gas.

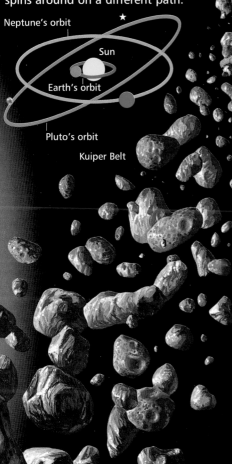

Odd orbit

Pluto takes 248 Earth years to go around the Sun. For 20 of these years it is closer to the Sun than Neptune is. While all the other planets orbit on roughly the same level, Pluto spins around on a different path.

Neptune's orbit

Sun

Earth's orbit

Pluto's orbit

Kuiper Belt

The Kuiper Belt

Beyond Pluto lies a huge ring of frozen rocks known as the Kuiper Belt. These drifting rocks did not merge into one of the planets when the Solar System was formed. Some astronomers think a few of them are bigger than Pluto.

Internet links

For links to websites where you can find out more about Pluto, go to **www.usborne-quicklinks.com**

Oort Cloud

Even farther away sits a huge, misty cloud, which may be made up of trillions of comets. This is called the Oort Cloud.

The Oort Cloud surrounds the outer edge of the Solar System like a vast, dusty ball.

Solar System

Bits and pieces

Our Solar System isn't just the Sun, the nine planets, and their moons. There are countless asteroids, meteoroids and comets flying around in it too.

Asteroids

Asteroids are big lumps of rocks and metal. Between Mars and Jupiter lies a large band of them, called the Asteroid Belt. The biggest one, named Ceres, is about 975km (605 miles) across. Some asteroids even have their own little moons.

Meteoroids

Meteoroids are smaller pieces of rock from space. Many are no bigger than a grain of instant coffee, but lots are larger. A few are as big as houses. Most burn up in the atmosphere as they fall to Earth, but some are too big to burn, and cause damage when they reach Earth.

Meteoroids that burn up in the sky are called meteors or shooting stars.

Meteoroids that hit a planet are called meteorites. This crater in Arizona, USA, was caused by a meteorite.

44

Comets

Comets are large balls of ice and dust. They come in from the outer edge of the Solar System to circle the Sun. Once past Jupiter, the heat from the Sun begins to melt the outer layer of the comet, and the solar wind blows a trail of gas and dust behind it.

Deep Impact

Scientists are working on a space probe named Deep Impact that will visit a comet called Tempel 1. It will blast a hole in the comet to try to find out more about it.

Part of the Bayeux Tapestry shows people looking at a comet in 1066. ★

A comet far away ★ from the Sun has no tail. It is just a solid block of dirty ice.

Closer to the Sun, ★ the outside begins to melt, and forms a trail of gas and dust.

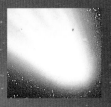

By the time it flies ★ by Earth the comet's tail is glowing. This makes it easy to spot.

This picture shows the comet Hale-Bopp when it passed by the Earth in 1997.

Internet link 🔍

For a link to the NASA website, where you can find out more about comets, asteroids and meteorites, go to **www.usborne-quicklinks.com**

The Universe

The Universe is everything in space. It is impossible to imagine how huge it is. Scientists think it is getting bigger all the time, so we will never be able to see to the very edge of space.

Light years

Space is so big that distances are hard to understand if you use normal measurements. Because of this, scientists describe space distances in "light years". One light year is the distance that light travels in one year.

A journey across the Universe

These pictures show what you would see if you could travel across the Universe in a spaceship. Start on the Earth (at the bottom of this page) and follow the numbers.

2 Here you reach the edge of our galaxy, the Milky Way, 90,000 light years away.

1 When you had passed the Moon and planets, you would reach the nearest stars, over four light years away.

Planets

The Moon

Earth

START

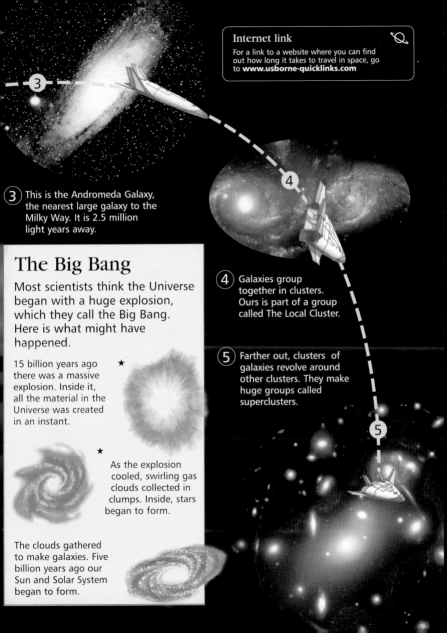

Internet link

For a link to a website where you can find out how long it takes to travel in space, go to **www.usborne-quicklinks.com**

(3) This is the Andromeda Galaxy, the nearest large galaxy to the Milky Way. It is 2.5 million light years away.

The Big Bang

Most scientists think the Universe began with a huge explosion, which they call the Big Bang. Here is what might have happened.

15 billion years ago there was a massive explosion. Inside it, all the material in the Universe was created in an instant.

As the explosion cooled, swirling gas clouds collected in clumps. Inside, stars began to form.

The clouds gathered to make galaxies. Five billion years ago our Sun and Solar System began to form.

(4) Galaxies group together in clusters. Ours is part of a group called The Local Cluster.

(5) Farther out, clusters of galaxies revolve around other clusters. They make huge groups called superclusters.

Distant suns

When you look up at the stars in the night sky you are actually seeing millions of distant suns. Stars only look tiny because they are so far away.

How big are stars?

Stars vary a lot in size. Here is how some other stars compare with our own star, the Sun.

Sun

Aldebaran

Rigel

Arcturus

Barnard's star

Star shades

Not all stars are white, although it is difficult to see this by just looking at the night sky. Some are red, or yellow or blue. You can see these differences much more easily in a photograph.

Below you can see stars in a part of the sky called the Sagittarius constellation.

White or blue stars are usually very bright and very hot.

Yellow stars, like our Sun, are usually cooler than white or blue stars.

Some of the largest stars are red. Compared to other stars they are cool.

Star clusters

Stars may look like they are scattered throughout the sky, but they hang together in clusters. This is because new stars are usually formed in groups, rather than singly. There are two main types of star clusters – open clusters and globular clusters.

This star formation is an open cluster. Stars in open clusters are usually bright and young.

The star formation below is a globular cluster. The stars here are older, and are gathered together more tightly than stars in an open cluster. Globular clusters can contain up to a million stars.

Internet link

For a link to a website with a clickable photo gallery from outer space, go to **www.usborne-quicklinks.com**

A star's life

Stars are being born here, at the top of this column of dust.

Stars are born, they shine, and eventually they die. Every stage of a star's life takes many millions of years.

Birth of a star

Stars are formed in a vast, swirling cloud of gas and dust called a nebula. You can see part of one here, called the Eagle Nebula. Below you can see how a star forms in a nebula.

1. Inside the nebula, clouds of gas form into dense clumps.

2. These clumps collapse inward to form a core which will become a star.

3. The core grows hotter and hotter.

4. The hot gas starts to explode, and the core begins to shine.

A middle-sized star, like our Sun, will shine for 10 billion years. Smaller star shine for longer. Massive stars shine very brightly, but burn out quicker.

The Eagle Nebula is so big it would take a ray of light a whole year to cross the area shown in this picture.

Death of a star

Eventually, a star's supply of gas runs out and it dies. This is what will happen to our Sun in around five billion years time.

1. Our Sun will become a Red Giant. This means it will swell up and turn red.

2. Gas on the outside will burn off into space.

3. A very heavy and much smaller ball, called a white dwarf, will be left.

4. The white dwarf will cool and fade away.

Supernovas

When stars much bigger than our Sun reach the end of their life, they explode. These explosions are called supernovas. Only four of them have been seen from Earth in the last thousand years.

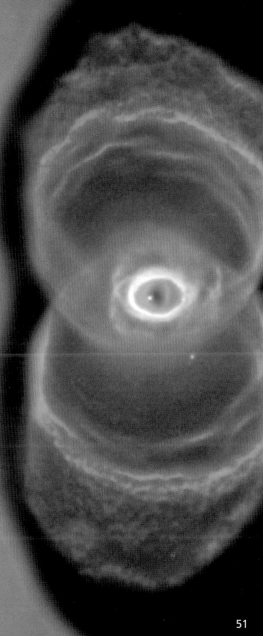

This dying star is the Hourglass Nebula. Rings of gas are blowing away from it.

Galaxies are collections of billions of stars, held together by gravity in one vast group. Most galaxies have a spiral shape, but some have a more scattered pattern. There are billions of galaxies in the Universe.

The Milky Way

The Sun is part of a galaxy called the Milky Way. It has over 100 billion stars, and is about 100,000 light years across. The Milky Way is not the biggest galaxy in the Universe, but it is much larger than many others. Like most galaxies it is spinning around a central hub. ★

Astronomers think the Sun and our Solar System are here.

A long trip

It takes 225 million years for the Milky Way to go all the way around. The last time our Solar System was in the same place in space that it is now, dinosaurs roamed the Earth.

The middle of the Milky Way is hidden by great clouds of dust.

If you could see the Milky Way from the side, it would look like a flat plate with a bulge in the middle.

Internet link

For a link to a website where you can find out more about the Milky Way and other galaxies, go to **www.usborne-quicklinks.com**

Galaxy shapes

Not all galaxies look like the Milky Way. There are several other galaxy shapes. You can see three of them on the right.

★ This type is known as an irregular galaxy. It doesn't have any real shape at all.

★ This round type is called an elliptical galaxy.

★ This type is a barred spiral galaxy.

Radio view

A kind of telescope called a radio telescope can "see" the Milky Way much more clearly than other kinds. The picture below shows the big bulge in the middle of our galaxy.

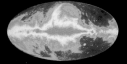

The red patch in this picture shows where most of the stars are in the Milky Way.

How many galaxies?

A hundred years ago astronomers thought the Milky Way was the only galaxy in the Universe. But over the last century, telescopes and radio telescopes have detected many millions of other galaxies.

This photograph shows some newly discovered galaxies. Before this picture was taken, astronomers thought there was nothing in this part of space.

Weird and wonderful

Far, far away in the depths of space, stars and galaxies are behaving in strange and amazing ways. Scientists have only recently invented telescopes and radio telescopes powerful enough to see such things.

This is a painting of what astronomers think a black hole looks like. It is sucking in everything around it.

A typical black hole is about the size of a town.

Everything near a black hole swirls around it, before it is sucked in.

Black holes

When some very big stars die, instead of fading away, they collapse in on themselves. Everything the star is made of packs down into a very dense ball called a black hole. The gravity of this ball is so strong everything around it, including light, is sucked into it. Black holes are invisible, but what goes on around them shows us where they are.

A jet of super-hot gas shoots out above and below the black hole.

Cosmic chaos

Everything in space is moving, and sometimes entire galaxies cross each other's path. The photograph on the right shows two separate galaxies, named the Antennae Galaxies, colliding. It takes millions of years for one galaxy to pass through another.

Cartwheel Galaxy

The photograph on the left shows what a galaxy looks like after it has collided with another. Astronomers call this the Cartwheel Galaxy, because a vast wheel-like circle of new stars has formed around its edge.

The blue parts of this galaxy show where new stars are forming.

Internet link

For a link to a website where you can find out more about black holes, go to **www.usborne-quicklinks.com**

Spinners

Sometimes a collapsing star makes a pulsar, rather than a black hole. As it shrinks, it spins faster and faster and becomes so dense, a piece the size of a sugar cube would weigh as much as 200,000 elephants.

As a pulsar spins, it gives off waves, or pulses, of tiny specks called electrons. These can be picked up by radio telescopes. The pulsar looks like it is flashing on and off.

There is a pulsar in the Crab Nebula.

The nebula lights up as it flashes.

Alien signals?

When scientists first detected pulsars they thought they had made contact with aliens. The regular beeps they picked up on a radio telescope sounded like messages from outer space.

Radio telescopes

Looking at the night sky

Although many of the pictures in this part of the book were taken using very powerful telescopes, you can still see many amazing things in the night sky just with your eyes.

Spiral galaxy

Milky Way

The Moon

Star cluster. This one is called the Hyades.

Old star. This one is called Betelgeuse.

This group of stars is called Orion.

This star is called Sirius. It is the brightest star in the sky.

These are some of the things you may be able to see without a telescope.

The Moon

The clearest sight in the night sky is the Moon. You can see it glowing brightly in the darkness because it is lit up by light from the Sun. As the Moon orbits the Earth it seems to change shape.

New Moon
When no light shines on the Moon, it is impossible to see it.

Waxing Moon
Gradually a sliver of light returns. The Moon appears to grow.

Full Moon
Once every 28 days all of one side of the Moon is lit by the Sun's light.

Waning Moon
As the Moon moves in its orbit less light falls on it. It seems to shrink.

What you can see

There is a lot to see in the night sky, if you know what to look for. Using just your eyes, you can see the Moon, stars, planets, shooting stars, comets and sometimes even spacecraft.

Stars

A clear night sky is full of stars. There are certain patterns you can look for. These patterns are called constellations, and there are 88 altogether.

This is a star pattern called Orion, which you can also see on the left-hand page. Ancient people thought this shape looked like a hunter.

This is a photograph of the constellation Orion.

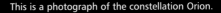

The Milky Way

This is what the Milky Way looks like on a very clear night. You can see it at certain times of the year if you are away from city lights.

Internet link

For a link to a website that has a good introduction to astronomy, go to **www.usborne-quicklinks.com**

57

Binoculars and telescopes

You can see plenty of things in the night sky with just your eyes, but you can see a lot more with binoculars or a telescope.

Binoculars

A good pair of binoculars is cheaper than a telescope. Binoculars are great for skywatching because they are light and easy to aim at the things in the sky that you want to look at.

This picture shows what a star cluster and three single stars look like through binoculars.

You use this focus wheel to make the image you are looking at sharper.

You hold on to the binoculars here.

Moon watching

Try looking at the Moon with your binoculars or with a telescope. You can see mountains, craters and flat "seas". Sunlight casts long shadows.

You look through these eyepieces. You can turn them to make the object you are looking at clearer.

Binoculars have two front lenses – one for each eyepiece.

Telescopes

Telescopes make things look much bigger than binoculars can. It's not worth buying a cheap telescope though. If you don't have a lot of money to spend, binoculars are a much better buy.

Here is the same star cluster and three single stars that you can also see on the facing page. A telescope makes them look bigger.

Internet link

For a link to a website with a useful introduction to buying binoculars or a telescope, go to **www.usborne-quicklinks.com**

Telescope tube

This is a small, low-power telescope. You use it to find things in the sky before looking at them with the big telescope.

The Andromeda Galaxy, seen with a telescope like the one on this page.

Galaxies

If you know where to look you can even see other galaxies with a telescope. They look like small misty patches of light. One of the easiest to see is the Andromeda Galaxy, which is two and a half million light years away from Earth.

You make your image sharper with this wheel.

This is the viewer for the big telescope.

This three-leg stand is called a tripod.

Space words

Here are some important space words which you'll find throughout this book.

alien a living thing from another world.

antenna the part of a radio where radio waves are picked up or sent out.

asteroid a rock orbiting the Sun. Thousands of them can be found in a part of the Solar System called the Asteroid Belt.

astronaut someone who goes into space.

atmosphere layers of gas that surround a planet or a star.

cargo bay area on a spacecraft, such as a space shuttle, where large objects such as satellites or parts of a space station can be carried.

cluster a group of space objects gathered together, such as stars or galaxies.

comet a chunk of dirty ice that orbits the Sun and can form a long tail as it melts. Comets sometimes come close enough to the Earth so that we can see them.

core the middle of a planet, moon, star or other space object.

crater a hollow on the surface of a planet, moon or asteroid, caused by something hitting it, such as a meteorite or asteroid.

day the time it takes a planet or moon to spin all the way around.

galaxy a group of hundreds of millions of stars held together by gravity.

gravity a force that pulls objects toward other objects. (Usually smaller objects to larger objects.)

laboratory a place where scientists do experiments.

light year the distance a ray of light travels in one Earth year. This is 9,500,000,000,000km (5,900,000,000,000 miles).

meteor a meteoroid that burns up in a planet's atmosphere. Also called a shooting star.

meteorite a meteoroid that hits the surface of a planet.

meteoroid dust, or small chunks of rock, in orbit around the Sun.

moon a mini-planet in orbit around another planet.

nebula an enormous cloud of gas and dust where new stars can form.

orbit the path of an object in space, as it travels around another object. For example, the Earth is in orbit around the Sun and the Moon is in orbit around the Earth.

planet a huge ball of rock or gas, which travels around a star.

radio telescope a type of telescope which uses radio waves to "see" objects in space. You can see pictures of some radio telescopes on pages 10–11.

robot a machine that can do a job in a similar way to a person.

rocket a type of engine in a spacecraft which uses exploding fuel to make it move.

satellite 1) something in space which orbits around something else. For example, the Moon is a satellite of Earth. **2)** an unmanned spacecraft which orbits the Earth.

solar panel a metal sheet used to gather heat from the Sun which can then be used to make electricity.

solar system a group of planets, and other objects, all in orbit around a sun. You can see a picture of our Solar System on pages 28–29.

solar wind a stream of tiny particles that blow off the Sun's surface and into space. When they pass by the North and South Poles of Earth they make the sky light up.

spacecraft (also called spaceship) a vehicle that is used to travel up to and in space. If a spacecraft has no people in it, it is unmanned.

space probe an unmanned spacecraft that collects information about objects in space.

space station a base in space, used for space exploration. You can see a picture of a space station on pages 18–19.

spacewalk when an astronaut in a spacesuit leaves a spacecraft and floats in space.

star a huge ball of exploding gas.

surface the outermost part of a star, planet or other space objects.

Universe everything that exists in space.

weightless when a person or thing in space appears to have no weight, and floats around.

year the length of time it takes a planet to travel around the Sun. Earth's year lasts 365 days.

Index

General websites

Picture credits